SPACE ALIEN
SPIKE

igloo

Spike was under attack. Three Scorpion Destroyers were closing in.

"Command to Pod 2! Command to Pod 2! Look out behind you!"

Spike's small Spacecraft shuddered as it took a direct hit.

Enemy fire came from all directions; above and below; to the left and the right.

The Galaxy lit up like a firework display.

Spike knew this mission to Planet Zodiac was a dangerous one - that's why he had been chosen to lead it.

He fastened himself into his seat and took control of the space cannon.

Then he steadied the ship. Spike had one missile left - this had to be perfect.

He pressed the 'FIRE' button and a torpedo rocketed towards the centre of Zodiac at the speed of light.

Kaboom!

"Take that, Space Fiends!" Spike cheered.

As Zodiac exploded into a trillion colourful pieces, the screen in front of him started beeping.

"Game Over! Game Over!" it flashed. Spike put down his controls. Just then there was a, knock on his bedroom door.

"I wish real life was as exciting," he moaned, loading his next game. "Come in."

His wish was about to come true . . .

"Who is it?" asked Spike, not looking up from his console.

He felt a tap on his shoulder.

As he spun around, Spike found himself staring at three very large and extraordinarily hairy aliens.

It was a family of Libran Monsters from the shattered Planet Zodiac.

The biggest of the Monsters bent down towards him and gurgled like a pan of boiling water.

It was a very strange language but Spike was able to understand it.

What he heard made him gulp.

"Because you have blown up our planet," the Libran told him, "your bedroom is going to be our new home."

Spike put down his games console. "You can't stay here! What will my mum and dad say? Not to mention the neighbours!"

"Well, that's not very fair," said the Monster. "After all, it was you who destroyed our planet."

While Spike and the Monster argued about what to do, the Monster's friends looked around the room for something to eat.

Socks, pillows, videos, calculators - one by one, they disappeared into the tummies of the alien visitors.

Spike had to act quickly.

"Try and stop them eating my room," he said to the leader. "I'll get them some real food from the kitchen."

But when he opened the door, another shock awaited him. Oddly shaped Aliens were tearing up the carpet, while others were pulling down the wallpaper and stuffing it into their mouths.

Spike didn't have time to stop. He just ran past them and down into the kitchen.

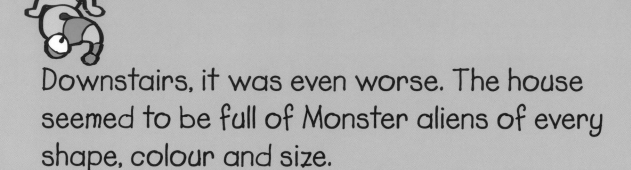

Downstairs, it was even worse. The house seemed to be full of Monster aliens of every shape, colour and size.

Spike held his hands over his eyes. "I've been invaded!"

Suddenly, there was a noise outside. Spike ran into the garden. He looked up.

"Oh no, The Intergalactic Space Police! Now I'm really in trouble."

Running back to the kitchen, he gathered packets of crisps and rounded the Monsters back up to his bedroom.

As he got back upstairs, he heard the Space Police enter the kitchen.

He dived into his room but the monstrous commotion was terrible.

"Quiet!" he shouted at the top of his voice. "You've all got to hide quickly. The Space Police are here."

The Monsters bumped into one another as they ran around looking for a place to hide. Spike tried to push them under his bed and into the wardrobe.

The smaller ones, he squeezed into drawers and the pockets of his dressing gown.

As he crammed the very last Monster under his lampshade, Spike turned off the light.

The bedroom door flew open. The room was flooded with a bright light. In the doorway stood the Space Police.

Spike was trapped. There was nowhere left for him to hide.

The Space Police took one step into the room and turned on the light..

"What on Earth have you been doing?" said his dad. "It looks as if there's been an explosion downstairs."

Spike stood with yoghurt round his mouth and packets of crisps in his hands. His pockets were bulging.

"Yes, there was an explosion," he said excitedly. "And then the house started to fill up with Monsters, who began to eat up the room, so I needed to get them some food. But when I got downstairs the Space Police turned up and the Monsters hid so I . . ."

"That's enough, space cadet," said his dad, shaking his head. "You'd better go and find them all again. Then they can help you tidy up this mess!"

also available...

Rude Roger   Dirty Dermot   Pickin' Peter   Space Alien Spike   Silly Sydney   Nude Nigel

Shy Sophie   Cute Candy   Royal Rebecca   Grown-up Gabby   Terrible Twins   Show-off Sharon